T0115331

dust in the
inner SONBEAM
aint

Carmine Sauchelli
& Nomde Guerre

WESTBOW
PRESS®
A DIVISION OF THOMAS NELSON
& ZONDERVAN

WestBow Press books may be ordered through booksellers or by contacting:

WestBow Press
A Division of Thomas Nelson & Zondervan
1663 Liberty Drive
Bloomington, IN 47403
www.westbowpress.com
844-714-3454

ISBN: 978-1-6642-2827-6 (sc)
ISBN: 978-1-6642-2826-9 (e)

Library of Congress Control Number: 2021906106

Print information available on the last page.

WestBow Press rev. date: 03/26/2021

NARRATOR UNO

So may I introduce to you-
Narrative for, 'Ireland', penned by Irsh mate.
Narrative for, 'Italy', penned by Italian paisano.

James Joyce had begun to turn over in his garden bower, that
i had been regurgitating medieval thoughts into, reading or,
rather editing my prattling attempts at putting bleach to the
fabric of what is known as society. My heart literally flutters as
if i chug-a-lugged a pure quadruple espresso from extra hyper
squeezed pouch of coffee beans, just thought glancing on this
issue along with the dice of destination. HEY, maybe my 'idea'
'heart' can be tamed of its abandoned caffeine cadence if I can
reach into Plato's forms and delete that which is the actual
real!!

And so, Submitted for your approval
I gathered up a co-author,{wink-wink}
Dual narrators furrowing into Dubliners incognito speaker
On the signpost up ahead
Where your next stop will unlock the door

You've just crossed over into into into e.e.cummings excursion
in the factory at horta de ebro while humming a Fay Victor
original.

However, there is typed at present—-DISCLAIMER— (all literature essentials WERE HARMED in the making of this picture)

Now back to pursuing the pages of our narrators isochronous logorrhea, which i tend to concede, well-nigh, with Josh Snodgrass who believed, "fewer words...effective communication...a quire of paper not squandered"...

.even so-they're guaranteed to raise a smile going in and out of style...

IRELAND-1

Ireland believed with fate-less foreboding that a some(one), anterior to me, might understand my heart and simplicity.

Adveniat Regnum Tuum.Hey, that's what catechism class instituted in my mind to recite. And for extra credit that would slice centuries off my purgatory purification all i had to commit was pay for a mass card, stoke a row of candles, and assist a lady, preferably an elderly elder, across the mall even if i had to force her off that store scooter she was so comfortably slouching into and carry her from Macys to the Applebees for the deed to be recorded. So, here's where Ireland looks over at Italy and speaks, "Yeah, you may think so, I have drunk now for twenty years come August 11, and am now a professional in a residual confessional." Italy and Ireland are sitting upon barstools in central/south Jersey. Ireland is rather aware that the brasciole (femine defined) have noticed him. Yes, as I deracinate' from my 'medigan' language(as Italy calls me), I do confess that this constant hanging with Italy has disembogues automatically- 'pisano' slang. He has been deemed a central producer of the pompatus of love at the local liquor store across the street. However, the owner of the joint knows and understands that Ireland is still, though not for long, in all probability, loyal to the mathair of his leanbh alainn. The mathair, having been an abusive and promiscuous woman albeit. Ireland is praying finally for certainty, recognition, love-you know, the pangs of sentiment outside the realm of this plain of pain,(Earth). Ireland again looks at Italy and speaks, "I am going to house you in p-ping-p-pong, you may have won the first round but this lefty is gonna beat you down." Ireland winks, "salut"!! Italy winks, "cent'anni !!" Ireland and Italy drain their mugs. Ireland's mam is dying. Ireland cries often. Ireland to Italy once again, "Here is a new composition that i am working on, one more tear and i'll pass out, I dropped two." Italy laughs lugubriously. Ireland responds cynically, "Cara mia, it was Lenin, the Russian Communist that was cynical, not John Lennon, the heart of the Beatles, you know.

IRELAND-2

I'll transpose his guitar to piano, play it finer, and then, play the guitar better than Lenin as I stare at my Pride and Prejudice protruding before my eyes pressed between 'A Spaniard in the Works' and 'The God Argument…' You know, it was 1968 when John Lennon penned/quelled/composed, 'Happiness is a Warm Gun', (tho) John might be in (Nevaeh) meant layers of images & song fragments but unfortunate irony saw future John in front of the devil's real warm gun

He/sea and guns were eventually killed for…murdered; comma, yo momma, obama, man. After all, I am humble and misconstrued, a literary 212. Never forget, you Sicilian, that an I.Q. is merely/simply a Faustian #, perhaps a cell phone # to call when that very viable, yet conspicuous I.Q.# places you in a cell, (from a cell, in a jail/gaol/gail, you cannot call a cell phone #. It is a cute facet/fact that i am loyal/ dying and yet will live to 105----

Now off to the ping-pong table!"

Ireland smiles. He is up quick and down with much eccentricity/ perturb ability. Italy prays, i'm sure mental maneuvering even still sitting at the bar- Ephesian 2:8-9(AMP) which is a hoisted imprint on his New Testament pocket edition, as usual in the general/at least major vicinity.

"G'hed, cuz--SERVE!"

ITALY-1

So

Where am i? Or, better yet, where was i?

Oh, of course -

where always

      I am

there

I was!! Unless there was a Sybil serenade that surfaced the threshold of consciousness like

Melville's Moby,

then I would wager the statistic and probability of my placement

      -other me-

Established with awe

Wadding the applied impasto of Monet's Impression, Sunrise.

Here i am, onward Christian soldier, jot and tittle pen dilapidating double edge sword. Advanced goggle stimulus.

      deviant retina pruned along caramel hue

      JUNCTURE JOLTS

Ireland's moisturized coaster, bantering slang, and manO e manO competition;

1) Coors Light promotion shadows the sole of his nostalgic chilled drinking vessel

nudged over the precipice to room temperature

only to succumb to the unbiased siege of gravity. 2) His malt &
hops pint salute, as if a glass surgical mask to resuscitate

Broadcast

All

Remaining beer into that 6 foot 5 frame!

ITALY-2

A frame that has corralled his opinion which is spewed forth through relativistic glasses, subjective preconceptions, & man made doctrines that has manipulated him to say(& think) that he is of 'The Way'-------------------- BUT,

he says&thinks this, when the bifocal absolute of Yeshua's objective special standard, reveals his lost soul, mauled and shackled in the dust of the wide road where the Temple's veil is still intact-

a frame - that also is mulched with an encyclopedic hemisphere of literature, almanac alertness, and Guinness Book of World records

(as Herman Munster said,["run, run, run"] run- on sentences) as his other plane of symmetry lies at the altar of the technical innovations of which Italy is enamored simultaneously with his Golden Calf called none other than- TA DA-

D{a}EDALUS!!

Although Italy possesses multi layered cultural, historical, artistic, grasping over and past Ireland by two decades(hey, the symbolism of the two countries is like a Snagglepuse cartoon- "Heaven's ta mergatroid, eeeven!!), Italy eases into the foxhole of soothing respect,

for the voice of Emerson etches into his white&grey matter as if on 'La Route' in the calm of Degas' lithograph whispering,

"In every man there is something wherein I may learn of him, and in that I am his pupil."

High Velocity's 'old school' jukebox, sanctions the Jersey Boys 'Sherry' to carom through the Camel exhaled haze. Yet my ardent neck tilts auditory availability

And Italy is able to process Ireland's proud victory lap of the mouth, "i, Ireland, has at least beat you this one game - me leafty-now that's right, i mean left, that's left not right but it's right what i did, i mean...?!"

"If you don't shudda u mouth, you're gonna see that i left, now that's 'right!!"

ITALY-3

One- W- in the win column from our ping-pong mini tournament is the only sweetness Ireland would taste after being paddle whipped. After all,a ten game win streak did consummate Italy the advantage. It was as if the 'B' side of Abbey Road was Italy's right hand and each game was the panting of songs where the old grooves-rendered no mercy, no rest, no breath.(grooves-remember LP's/ 45's---hey G-Pa, what's that black round thin hard frisbee in the crate in the corner of the attic?) Italy's head

BOB

    B

      L E

            S with acknowledged courtesy. AH, but here's the rub- Hamlet---------does Italy's friend and over all good guy, heed the shy smirk of this Italian-American's labium oris. Superius fleshly heritage from Calabria, inferius(defined as other half!--not being 'inferior in status) from Sicilia!!! Can the occupied boasting tongue of Ireland decipher, that, maybe, perchance to dream, That saccharine was the actual ingredient and not pure cane? That his one solitary win was my pity gift like the rare debut along the 'AT' of Stokes Forest of a broken spectre causing Flora's babble to Mr. Clennam while intermittently reciting Coleridge;

"The viewless snow-mist
Weaves a glist'ning haze
Sees full before him,gliding
Without tread,
An image with a glory round its
Head.."

Well, onto the topic. VERITAS. Wow, i bet Aletheia is jealous she's not mentioned here also but,now,now, we can't have a cat fight no matter how sultry in hypotheticVILLE between this Greek and Roman and their mediterranean healthy tans.

VERITAS! DOMINATES!

ITALY-4

MY ENHANCED THOUGHT PREACHING commences as heard by my soul sitting in that non-denominational pew - YO Ireland ....You need to be a Branch

Grafted into the true Vine and then the fruit from the Branch will be visible and delicious but if there's NO fruit then (DUH) you're NOT a Branch!! Because from what i judge,

OOOHH,yes, that's right, I said it!! How dare i judge! ESPECIALLY, with the PC police now in vogue With their 2+2=5 mantra--- right- WRONG!! Hey, listen/heed since your eternity depends on it!

Yeshua commands us to judge- judge righteously. So, me-judging- from over 30 years of 66/40 coursing through the veins of my being, i have all the credentials and authority from my Master to judge!

How did Italy apply his gift of the Spirit- to peel no fruit- shuck no Branch- display no Christian- unveil no heaven(hence hell bound)-

One simple question! Through tough thorough thought though-

where is the scriptural address of where the Lion/Lamb grants His Branch-His Sheep a new name written on a white stone??

If the answer is anything other than the 2+2=4 absolute(recollect, Italy received the 2+2=5 relativistic answer from his amico) then it would be as if a Beatle fanatic was not able to shout out the names of the Fab Four-John,Paul,George,Ringo or was not able to flaunt before all web site, magazine, or conversational surveys that, Sgt.Pepper(Revolver,Rubber Soul, 'White' Album, Abbey Road for that matter) is the most influential, musical, artistic, ground pulverizing, creative, innovative, album EVER, and if they were incapable, then they might as well have posed as Rodin's 'Thinker" among the plane wreckage of Patsy Cline!!

-proverbial Solomon says,'Better is open rebuke than love that is concealed.'(PRV27:5NIV)

Per Favor Ireland- do not wade in a Hubris stew because you might dive head first into that burning pot alongside Milton's Lost antagonist!

IRELAND-3

D{a}eadalus?? A perforation into/unto the musterbation/monstrom is key, (hey Heresy), and it unseemingly/unflinchingly seems, (don't flinch now, cuz!), that Ireland's humility, tho' propitiates in mate's (1st) installment has been questioned. Iconic...Iconic. Francesco Forgione Pio, St.Augustine, St.Therese of Lisieux, -no-Ireland/County of Mayo is certainly not Catholic, right? He/I, (and this couldn't possibly be an autobiographical account), is just a simple...simplistic...superlative man; posthumously so, whatever you've known is thrown to the wind... akin to begin anew, and why not, we'll get to that-more sin; read the THREAD-bread the bread! There are many myths about Ireland, "That ol' poetical prattler", "That deviant/defiant/dangerous sot", "Maniacal/manipulative spiritual murderer", "Daddy', "godfather-in the religious Catholic sense", 'Uncle", "step-dad', "womanizer","Socio/Psychopath". Hey/ you readers- hay/you horses, Tom Waits, Joyce, cummings, Benicio Del Toro, James Douglas, Malachi,Shaman, Dionysius, Morrison, and the saints that have gathered together for this Velocity program, they, in the least, understand what is true,... Veritas. Firstly, Jesus. Secondly, children. Thirdly, women. Ireland and Italy simmer/soothe through the Velocity program, shy smirk, tho' Italy seems to believe that Ireland is possessed of the pomp. Naturally, Ireland is aware of Italy's 10-1 lead and the occasional smirk and perhaps, the ersatz superiority. We shall see, you see,Ireland,is merely a simple man.Did i mention that i am drunk right now? In 1967, the Doors, Velvet Underground with Nico and Warhol tried, failed attempt to paddle whip the Sergeant in the face with a pepper. After all, nada y pues nada,our nada who art in nada but you can't escape a clean well-lighted cafe. Have you heard(it through the grapevine{Gaye/CCR version],that Ireland will play Prince's guitar on the piano? As if Sir Prince,(one of the finest guitar caresser (add in Setzer), has anything on Ireland acoustically, nylon humility. I luv ya cuz! Now, to retread above-count backwards 16-ish lines to the word-THREAD-and here is where i show Italy i know of the Creator-Voila—THREAD

IRELAND-4

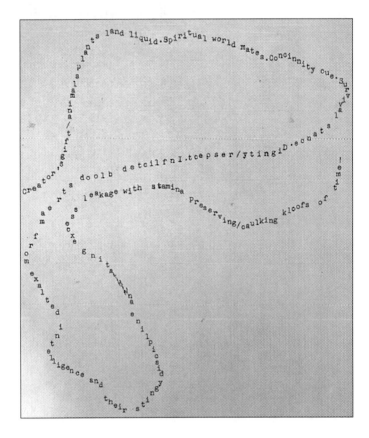

ITALY-5

IPod (actually not yet 4 me)- You Pod- They Pod-Black/Blue Berry-MP3-Web/Net-FB-Instagram(the 'gram can't wait)Twitter/ Fritter(apple,YumYum eat 'em up,weepwaaa)...& so forth with the conjugation----

STOP!!!

--use you mind

man/woman, 4(not only) God's sake BUT 4 the sanity of your imagination.

Get back(no-not Tucson Arizona)2 basic reading, A LA MODE,d

> r
> i
>   p
>   p
>   i
>   n g
> raw Dickens

cool cream on warm Victorian pie. Or, sail across the Atlantic(to be where you belong)

and Breathed with Emily in her second floor bedroom

Beguiled of immortality over a naive Main Street that was monitored by a diminutive square stand- epic desk reaching beyond the restraint of its small space--- Dawdle in the Swaddle of pink flowered-

as'twere a bright Bouquet paper enthralled to the wall only by the Immured friendship of-

-quatrains-triplets-couplets-as the Lightning balm of iambic rhythms-slanted-partial and some - faintly off-

Sweet hoisted with Summer miracle of -dashes-CAPS- Spiciest syntax- obtained flavor from her Piercing function-BEING-

Now
Don't put (her) Thread and Needle-
    memory trace
Leave (her) Needle in the Furrow-
    floorboard realm
From then- Dreaming of her sewing
        Auxiliary dress pockets to gather genius lyrics- designful
            jottings of
                an unconventional reserved soul-

-- BROADWAY BLADDER TIME--
so during our theater-lude

                        we go to our reporter in the field
                                        actually
                        the FLANEUR on the wall---
                            "Mr.Flaneur,hi, this is

Ms.Reporter,excuse me,hello,excuse me, I know your proboscis is like very busy,ah, inhaling off the wall that broken down mush piece of pizza, which is giving me agita just glancing at you, but what's your exploration of these two?"

ITALY-6

"Well,MsReporter,

Italy corresponds the non-offensive profile Guido traits;

Nervous exploring hands-

'Yo/Che Se Dice' speech-

Legion of cousins-

Holiday&Sunday core conventions-

Epicurean leftovers-

Wooden spoon frontier intimacy-

Sonorous diction-

half DNA from da Boot/half from da Island next 2 da Boot-
however- spanked as a newborn full in Newark, NJ.

Now- his friend is definitely goo-goo eyes 4 abstract a-takzhe
graffiti neo-expressionist in the previous pages of his expression(of
which, by the way- Italy is definitely on board with those stares)-
however his DNA spanked as a newborn full from the Emerald
traits of Eire corresponds the non-offensive;

With strong roots in Saint Brigid's Cross-

Active Pub culture & jigs & reels & step/ceili dances-

Sessions of clairseach with hospitable handshakes-

A stable potato diet while riveted on Gaelic football & rugby-,"

"Ah,Mr.Flaneur I don't mean to be rude but i'm gonna be obsolete from this interview very shortly so we need to wrap this up.Is there any more observations you'd like to report?"

"Yes, it seems that Ireland has a blurry perception dazed with facial contortions from Italy's cell phone interruption with one of his pisano's relating to

- Il Dibattito Italiano in Casa-
GRAVY or SAUCE?? done -now let me get back to regurgitating."
Yo you
Yes you
Oh perceiver of these premeditated grammatical mind talk
You shoulda been there
Oh
Wait
You are there
Here
So keep those fingers from obliging the keyboard's alliance
Dispose the top off your lap
Persevere to indulge manifold ink on2 your thoughts.
Alright-enough of the #'s, i"ll use letters 4, i mean,'for' their proper usage.

Now back to our Kabuki

Nah, just goofing, back to our opera-Scaramouche Scaramouche Galileo Galileo
Figaro Magnifico

Oh, Mamma Mia Mamma Mia

Easy come Easy go

As we go back to the local patrons who

Localize

Before their choice of marathon HD(3D-R2D2) sports motioned

extra thin screens.

And there

ITAY-7

mingled among the routine

a former co-worker

Slices-Dices past beer poster walls fringed with rows of old- school

pinball dinosaurs

Lauding

Latrine

Lathered

Language

"!!#%**><+^^!!hey, Italy, long time, what's new?"

"Ahh,nothin',just the thirteenth letter of the Greek alphabet!!"
Inarticulate response muted by the ignorance of the ancient
Hellenistic pronunciation of Nv(pronounced-NEW).
"Right, ah, well whatever, gotta go. Got Yankee tickets. Later. Go
finish your game."

And so

Ireland with his fury eyebrows crashing from the curiosity of my

old acquaintance

Balances

Then cajoles

The conversation back his way while his words maraud along
the dark skin of a receding Winchester. "Saints! This saint that
and that saint this. From St. Ann to St.Therese to St. Zita.I ask,
knock,seek. Please help me find this. Please protect me and my

family from that.What should i do about this or that. Oh, wait, Italy, you don't believe in saints!!"

"NO no no," my eminent chastisement from this accusation and gross misinterpretation of the word 'saint', hoisted Italy's iconoclastic rank pleasing the Lord with the following refrained diatribe(which will not set well with the Boys near 7 hills),

"Obviously I believe in saints- the term/topic is in the Bible.So, we need to define saints based on the only standard from which we receive the definition, principle and example of that word. And there's only one meaning applied to the word without any hint of any other interpretation, and that is- SAINT- in scriptures- is a person, dead or alive who first when aalive was born from God and was a lover, follower, child of the FatherSonHolySpirit, being 'born again' as a saint and remaining a saint even after death. You know there's no problem to glean scriptural doctrine or historical efforts of the saints

But
To petition prayers to
Or focus attention to
Or consciously converse to
Well,well,
VENI VIDI WEE WEE!!

That's my excretion sentiments especially when humans, who are dead, clueless and deaf to earthly material affairs - are-

Canonized, beautified, and godified

By the white zucchetto triple tiara wearing Papa or when they're summoned along the beads of chanting fingers

VENI

VIDI

WEE WEE

and add plenty of muck!"

ITALY-8

-Diatribe(minus the lemon peel pucker)

A prolonged Diatribe promotes

For righteousness-

> "There is only ONE propitiated crown of thorns thrust into the scalp of only ONE Mediator.

So,

the question comes down to

who is your Master? Because

the only uncaused Cause

the only uncaused Master, says that there is only ONE mercy

seat where everyone should focus and bow in reverence and awe!

as in water face reflects face, so the heart of man reflects the man.(Prv 27:19) Do not (REPEAT) do not participate, do not have fellowship with the unfruitful works of darkness but rather expose/rebuke them. (Eph 5:11) Whosoever says i know Him but does not obey Him-His commands- or does not walk IN His light, is a liar and the truth is not IN him. (1 John 1:16/2:4) The greatest of man's power is the measure of his surrender. Be a real man-- man-- and hopefully the distance you surrender is far enough to lift the standard of Ephesians 2:8-9(AMP) reflecting the Son's light

to extinguish all dark statues,relics,religion,reliance,self,satan and
society."

            non-sequitur

            interlude--ur

                vivid sprawled snow

                    welcomes the reveling wonder and

                      excitement

                          bonus winter scene

predestined boy

organized

upon vintage toboggan torso

cozy clasped to pet tiger,

            "It's a magical world Hobbes ol' buddy... let's go

            exploring."(Watterson's last entry)

                ZOOM

                Panel

                Comic genius

                ZOOM   ZOOM

                        Panel - exit- like

                        the smooth charming

                        baritone vocals and

        Cheerful casualness of the King of Cool-

SWAY INTO Italy-9

ITALY-9

Ireland constrains the USA-made paddle

Basic ping-ping requirements

-satisfied-

and hydroplanes the shrieking Winsome Counter Saddle Bar Stool(nano second recognition)

there

Liquor laced linoleum looms the inconspicuous destination of this quadruple legged solid beechwood. The sauntering hope of victory wafts between jade ovals like the aroma that tempts the youthful memory of that virgin slice of boardwalk pizza- Jersey style-

- attainable(YEA)contemplatively-

- reality (NAY) unattainable -

He's prepped for another superfluous attempt to defeat the almost, should I dare compare-

the Bruce Lee mastery of Italy's Jeet Kune Do speed and dominance in game 12 through 16.

I will definitely admit that i'm enthralled and totally enjoying his competitive courage and ability which sparks my reflexe juices and actually executes saline droplets out from my forehead holes.

But

Before the border net of this sporty table is actively caressed by both of these yo-yo'z, Italy gently and lovingly desires repentance from

Ireland. Of course solely motivated by the 'Great Commission' and decides to obey and sprinkles out the bait, "Well, will you remove the deceiver's blinders and bathe ONLY in the light of Ego Eimi!"

Ireland debates with himself whether to respond and one of his selves losses the dispute, "Ah, I kinda understand what you're incinerating,i mean, insinuating... but I'm basically a good person...i attend church during the holidays... I'm not like Hitler..."

UNfortunately
Not the answer of conviction that would
HACK Agag to pieces
And so dear friends and friends of friends
It's more like a

> Hitler to Neville response, "Das Sudentenland,
>   jetzt reicht e saber fur mich."

Anyway
Back in the day
What invaded my city of broken down walls was Dewars&Bud and crimson nostrils from powered straw interruption on a weekly foundation
However
Jesus
Grace
Is sufficient and the Angel of the Lord encamps an eternal impenetrable fort around me

Oh

And did i mention

I'm not drunk!

Heart central to Ireland, come in mate. Luv ya cuz!!

-remember- love is not a feeling or even verbalization but an act
of the will-

IRELAND-5

Ireland, would be/could be gigolo- "Man zahlt und du must tanzen", will not go to hell on account of his loyalty and responsibility. Ireland has taken accountability/culpability for the thangs and pangs that he hath caused others even if he hasn't caused them. "Competition is naught.I say nien to trivial competition. As do you, Italy, cuz, did we, mention to Ms. Nameless Bartender that we have chosen this/her salon to compose the next, "Dubliners"? How about, Cask of Amontillado"?-- Innamorada? Did she give me her numbuh? Never forget Dylan Thomas! The publishers didn't ascertain that he was a drunkard until he appeared with the hidden pretense of being un-inebriated.Winchester cigar Wrath/Love/Dichotomy. Ireland is tired,lad; tired of being loyal. He misses his child.

Who's on 3rd? No Who's on 1st! Who gets the check? Absolutely. So, Absolutely gets the check? NO-WHO!! Hold the cross and do not hit anybody! Frame-a frame Schopenhauer quelled of Will, and hence Nietzsche; bygones. Love, love, love, screamed/bellowed Morrison,cajoles and private still in pants private, arrested in Dade county as having been lewd. "No Woodstock for the True Soulful/Bluesy Snoopy! Goodnight, Jim, you beautiful poet." Italy knows Ireland is drunk now! Ireland to the bartender after the termite walked into the bar and asked, "is the bar-tender here?",

"Beefeaters on the rocks, 3 olives, 1 lemon, the bill in Latin, please, thank you, and you're very welcome; am I an imposition?"

Ireland drains the drink and saves the olives for Mrs. Peter Griffin. Italy drops off Ireland in Quahog. Stewie has finally disposed of all of Brian Griffin's snausages and Ireland drop-kicks Stewie from Rhode Island to the River Jordan. Presently, is there a bar called, 'High Velocity', and if so, why do they not have/possess any Lennon/Lenin/McCartney/McCarthy songs in their technologically advanced jukebox? Ireland is at his mother's home, smoking cigarettes incessant(ly), inefficacious(ly), and inexorab(ly) by himself, musing about Winnie the Pooh(hahaheheherherLOL-that word Pooh-forces giggles). You will not shoot your psalms tonight St. John Wilkes Iscariot?

Perhaps, perchance to dream, i do need a rub

, but perhaps Italy is correct and a self-imposed petard perchance will lead him to the fire that ceaseth not and where the worm dieth not. Ireland looks to his quill, "no, i cannot ascribe to such an impiety. Jesus is Just-Merciful-and above all, He is Love"! Ireland prays for the Moment, Lord, like the deicide's dove, that Moment, O Lord, when he may exhale and rest in the True Merciful and Divine Justice and Love of Christ. Eventually when my tour/chore of purgatory is merited, only then the Judge that Ireland has ever paid any soulful heed to will release him-(i hope). It is all anterior and superior, and all in the Lord's fiat.

With that unwritten, Ireland takes a long pull of coffee and smiles,

"Anyway,you women who have thus far destroyed me, you cannot handle me, I implore thee,beseech thee, I beg thee to try to buy my idiosyncrasies, watch me adore thee as i apply kindness to your sighs, you see(s), I please to seize with ubermensch overman kinder-than betterman, I'm not crass,so upper/lower class that is to rhyme, so do not let me sin, I was simply attempting to edit, however, I let,run,run,run, and i took a drag(groovy-remember lets try and resurrect that word-groovy) or 20, I would kiss you and you would either end up, pregnant, or, with cancer.?"

Ireland cracks open a good cheap beer and prays for his women, everybody, the Lord, and Italy's entire paisano family--------------

DONE,

IRELAND-6

NOW AFTER

> genuflect petitions before El Santo Padre's sanctioned
> terracotta
> Ireland finally scans Italy's perpetrated placed verse/terse
> on my
> oak soak cafe table

tessellated with Druid acorns
embedded as a tease from the surface
a decor so near yet so far
unable to eat-

> bummer-now I can't merge with the wisdom of
> this mighty tree,so i tarry/nary, but here goes

I quote his poem-
'Nectar of Thundershower Splash,
Kitten sojourned in a spool's avalanche
Serene paste!
Child swarmed in a toy's fiction
Praline taste!
Grass volleyed in a wind's review
Sordine haste!
Grizzly larking latent smiles transforms

Amputating claws-Crushing paws-Cotton caress-Architectural finesse of cubs rumpus!

Hazy arms of handless beams parry through a barricade of leaves to the wrinkling glass-

Spreading like a fan tracery.

A marriage of the wind!

Prompt intimacy

Instant conception--TWINS BURST--In a miraculous creation of being!

Then-one/simpers

a mesmerizing glitter

And -it's/sibling winks a glare

Harvesting pirouettes

Boundless

A pond not uttered!

Into dulcet eyes silence fury's immense

To anyone who's focused. Evidence of things unseen, in a vault of real

Perceptions considered

That is to conquer mundane facades.

Dexterous Splash

Refulgent mountains, of the Ancient Of Days' radiant ornamentation

Dainty slopes

Gestural gardens

Adorned

In the dictum of sweetness!' ------

Oops-------

The brewer's yeast from the creamy land of Guinness strains/
STAINS

---oops--- Italy's page-oops

. What/watt will i tell him??

Ah, I'm positive he has a buttress copy in his old school file cabinet
but to be safe i'll blame Marley's reggae ska 'Rocksteady' or in this
scenario-- 'UNsteady' (source- my Viking beer mug mixed with
my extreme tiddly balance and NO i'm not smartcell thumbing)!

ITAY-10

The cruise back from Quahog was Italy's hush-hush time,
although it was at times,

                    tumultuous.

It was the quiet of times   the

                tumultuous

                   of times! Co-exist? Punctuation symbol,

                   hovering over your head,

for these times.

Yes,

Cartoon people

The interrogation point

To make the point!!

Sure

At one moment

Quiet!

Then

Tumultuous! **SURE**- and speaking of,i mean typing, this
homonym,come on down/ up/across to the **SHORE!**

Jersey- that is. Hey,taste our tomatoes and cultures and history.
While you're here-you

heed/need to meets/Keats;

A thing of beauty is a joy forever;
Its loveliness increases;it will never
Pass into nothingness;but still will keep
A bower quiet for us,and a sleep
Full of sweet dreams,and health,and quiet breathing.

Before the glacier stretch of sand at Wildwood Crest mocks two supposedly athletic legs, Italy exits the proud Garden State PKWY at 140 with a punctilious embrace of his hometown.

Ex officio founded 1666!!

A slithering merge of competent reflexes pivots into 280 east and eventually a sigh is spied. I spy, St.Rose of Lima grammar school(that's what we&they called grades 1-8 back in the day) and close enough so that you can hear the priest taking an extra sip of wine during Mass-there- gothic-ish church and stained glass windows to the upper left or north from the highway, where many student lunches were accidentally(on purpose) tasted by Italy and Ireland, unbeknownst to their uniformed sanctioned academic preoccupied minds, way back in the day 'cause all lunches were tossed into the closets in the hall out of view from the classrooms. Now, no sooner than you can say, "where did those days fade to?", my easterly direction halts onto First&Orange streets. Downtown's partial skyline devours the lingering gasp

as the flashback of city scampering,sauntering, and savage gutter wisdom vivifies the ebullience of my dance.

Traffic luminous. Dangling high. Evasive mute. Severe red. Taut covenant. Eye ebb to brain ebb to will to

STOP! Then a convergence, a shot gun convoy of miscellaneous entrepreneurs.

"Heyya mista,wash ya windshield?"

"Jo'mon,buy sum condy, mon?"

"Dude, need the Star Ledger?" The green is rewarded as the dominant color.Sorry boys, no currency exchange today.Besides just packing plastic. The beepbeeps blurt even before a hint of my foot touched the accelerator! Mod'awn- don't clog your arteries stunadz!

ITALY-11

Hunger allies with a grumbling pugnacious paunch,which inconspicuously creeps over the confines of a black&brown Navajo leather belt.Anticipation fashions itself into a gathering group

like the positioned dash of passengers at the subway station on Park Ave

.OHHHHHHHHhhh

aaaaaaaaahhhhhh,succulent,oh yeah- there it is!!(and i'll describe 'there' after approx 3 sentences)

Italy allocates his direction through Branch Brook Park

where

to the immediate right-- the eyes are granted the blessing to gaze at

the bank of the landscaped itsy bitsy(no nursery rhyme to chime-sorry) 'Old Blue Jay' lake which is still protected by two cement lions gallantly ceased from any motion as if awaiting the chant from the Schantz pipe organ of the Cathedral Basilica. Mapacha simba-yeah-they're still there after decades of chasing the next century, and from my perspective they've been there since the dawn of my birth and especially since I became aware of their stance when my dad routinely pushed&released us(me/my sisters/cousins/friends) to the smirk of gravity as we forged through the mountain white on vintage sleds that weighed twice our body mass from metal frames that made iron proud. Of course, the mountain that was

-then-

Is,

now a small hill

which is from my perspective or any adult for that matter a small hill

but for the child in us,it will remain a mountain and of course from the child's perspective it is a mountain-

now!

Ok- here is the 'there' I promised to describe approx 3 sentences prior-

Oohhhhhhhhh-ahhhhh

Succulent-

TONY'S HOT DOGS !   TONY'S HOT DOGS!!

'There' They are-here we are-

push cart disciples

Bowing before the famed 4 wheel altar

As Petitions curl along the savory steam to be answered definitively by the petitioner as proclaimed;

"five hot ones with kraut,per favor,light on the mustard."

Behind me, blue,green,white,rainbow collars- hard,soft, & fire hats, badges seen and concealed. Barringer students & teachers, common & uncommon folk. All devious in unusual unplanned unison ravaging lip tongue moisture alertness for some homemade utopian recipes to satisfy the cheeks and hope the drip and stain dry enough to be able to taste the next day. Italy ventures the indiscernible depths of the park but not before he stuffs George into a crowded 'tip' jar(and for you literalist don't you dare knock it over). The cogent public seat premiers a splattering of pigeon Picasso musings. The assail of home concocted

lava onion sauce on a teary palate was not enough of a deterrent for the revival of Ireland

cloistered to my thoughts.

Be careful of real perceptions of unreality

Be careful of real perceptions of unreality

-line stutter for your attention-

ITALY-12

Be careful of real perceptions of unreality- like,when you really perceive the sun's slothful climb up over the eastern horizon-up-up-up, all the way to high position-noon- high noon(classic movie), and then with a slothful dip down-down-down, fading behind the western divide

but as Aesop's dog snatched for the phantom meat gazing into the river's rippling mirror and lost the reality to a passing raven it is the earth's axis that gathers for us

the intervals of light and dark!

I press onward and hand over all accolades and glory to the Blessed Trinity for Their gift to me-

DISCERNMENT

And as Martin Luther responded at the Diet of Worms, "unless I'm convinced by the testimony of the scriptures or by clear reason,for I do not trust either in the pope(and I add Iman,Rabbi,Guru, false Televangelist,etc) or in councils alone, since it is well known that they have often erred and contradicted themselves.I am bound by the scriptures I have quoted and my conscience is captive to the word of God. I can not and will not retract anything, since it is neither safe nor right to go against conscience. May God help me."

My scriptural antennae and biblical bifocals will relate to Ireland's prior faith based statements and anyone who confesses like him with Mark 7:6-7(NKJV&AMP)(when Jesus says),"These people honor Me with their lips but their hearts are far from Me, in vain they worship Me teaching as doctrines the commandments and traditions of men."

Now before I begin,

I'm stating

Clearly

That my goomba/mate

Ireland

If he died in the state he's in right now(and I don't mean NJ)

He would go directly to hell

Not heaven.(my reasoning and scriptural evidence will ensue -soon) BUT LET ME STATE

Categorically

That as long as he has breath

He still has a chance through grace by faith to enter heaven

But only

IF

He repents, submits and obeys all the scriptural clues and the map laid out for him so far.Now back to Ireland's statements of incrimination. Even plain old common sense logic dictates and exposes Ireland's contradictions, bad fruit and tares. He honors with his lips and his heart is a theological stone of verbatim, and I quote, " Jesus is just. Merciful, love and divine justice and the only Judge."

BUT{and I don't mean glutaeus maximus}(oh,stop it you,you homonym ears) he believes and hence,worships,based on the commandments and traditions of man,posterior/anterior of how Yeshua says one enters heaven and not hell and he does this with a capital 'I' moral boast as all accolades are to self and his own merits which tack him to the tree on Golgotha by saying, and again Italy quotes with a slight paraphrase incorporated, "I will not go to hell on account of my loyalty and following through on my responsibilities."

I ask-
Loyalty to who? Responsibilities for what?
Of course he's completely dealing on a horizontal human plane.

ITALY-13

Now,

For salvation

For heaven

He

MUST

Be dealing on the vertical supernatural plane-

> GOD
>
> Relationship
>
> Direct
>
> Personal!! Eating His flesh-drinking His blood(no-not the wafer/wine kind)DAILY!

until

Sola Scriptura

Sola Fide

Sola Gratia

Sola Cristos

are the anthem of his(anyone's) heart, mind, soul, strength AND he(you) can humbly yet boldly enter through the veil into the Holy of Holies and KNOW and BELIEVE and LOVE Christ, the Father and the Holy Spirit and be able to quote what Their Word has revealed and be a doer not just hearer solely based only from Scriptural standards, principles, doctrines and examples. Other than that- he(you) can say he(you)believe all he(you) want but that dont mean he's(you're) saved/going to heaven, after all,in the book of James chapter 2 verse 19 he(you) can read the following;'even the demons believe and tremble'!(NKJV)

Does that make them Christians and are those demonic fallen angels worshipping spending eternity in heaven??

NOT!! Again

Even if they typed 'Thread' and mentioned the Creator fringed with some truth, is Jesus precious in heart pulse??

In Matthew 7:21-23, Jesus says;"not everyone shall enter the kingdom of heaven who says to Me,'Lord,Lord,did not we prophesied,cast out demons and done many wonders in Your name,but only those who do the will of My Father.I will declare to them, 'I never knew you,depart from Me, you who practice lawlessness."(NKJV)

To test and examine IF you're in His will means that your standard,principle,doctrine,example, response- flows from the knowledge, love, belief, obedience out of the gospel/scripture which is the power of God for Salvation-ALL-ALL

only/solely based on Jesus merit as you/me/everyone knows, believes, trust ONLY-ONLY, Jesus as your personal UPER! (come people, now, research the Greek- B-A-Berean!)

As I sacrifice my innards to the encouraging chant of - "just two more and smother those dogs with the inability to breathe from the blaze of onions!",a conversation protrudes sporadic through the distant formal cries of Engine 15 & 9's nutritious valor;

Customer 1- "they say you can't talk about religion or politics. Well, first of all, who are 'they'? Don't always listen to 'they'! Second of all,it's not that you can't talk but it's the swollen infection of ignorance-pride-relativism-and the puss of podsnappery and of course the slant of the media's biased propaganda or a.k.a. 'fake(deceptive narrative)news'-i mean really,no O'Reilly, they're NOT journalists anymore but political activists.However i need to NOT commit the fallacy of 'parts to whole' and admit that it's not ALL of the media just when they fall into the category as i described above."

ITALY-14

Customer 3(customer 2 withdrew his consent to participate)-"Obama this,Obama that-yeah i didn't vote for him and many of us who are offended by what HE DOES or doesn't do and when we voice objection to his policies they call us racist. Dude-- it's not a matter of race,although they keep whipping out that card, as if other races were never enslaved or attacked by racism as if their own race didn't enslave themselves or as if they weren't prejudiced against their own 'people'. Just go to some African tribes when they have different food tastes or traditions or land and they decide to fight each other even if they're of the same race.They enslaved each other. These revisionists spew worm ulcers as truth but we need balanced history and Schaeffer's 'True Truth'. The Arab Slave Trade was hundreds of years before the Trans Atlantic Slave Trade.sure whites enslaved blacks but muslims enslaved whites and blacks and in some Islamic countries it continues till today and an offspring of that was the Barbary slave trade from the 16th -18th century enslaving almost 2 million whites-mainly from European areas and its coast lines..also lets not forget that most of the slaves sold to the Arabs and 'Europeans' or Colonist were captured and sold by african blacks selling their own kind for money or trade.Fredrick Douglas/African abolitionist Ottobah Cugoano/Ugandan President Yoweri Museveni/Ghana Diplomat to UN Kofi Awoonor/Civil Rights Nigeria congress-ALL admit accuse/are ashamed/blame those African leaders in their guilty primary role of causing selling their own black people into slavery. Also in the colonies and when it became America free blacks enslaved blacks! Native Americans enslaved blacks. Whites were enslaved by the natives.Thousands of white Irish were sold by England to different areas in the New World as slaves from about 1640-1830 Let's not forget the slaves of Assyria, Babolyn, Greece Egypt,Rome,Portugal,Spain,Aztecs,Mayans,Incas and the list goes on and on. Many of those empires incorporated slavery intheir systems for hundreds of years. Now just a side note- as far as slavery in 'America' we need to remember 'America' as a country with its constitution/bill of rights/checks&balances was formally declared 'the United States' 9/9/1776.So with that in mind 'America had slavery for only 87 years before abolishing it thanks to Lincoln, the abolitionist and many white Americans(and note-i'm not advocating slavery for even a second) but note- 87 years and thanks to our glorious nation/ constitution and men like Lincoln it took only 87years to abolish slavery and unfortunately we had a civil war to also push it through. HATE=PREJUDICE=racist=HUMAN NATURE!! If anyone thinks there is perfect individual humans anywhere anytime constant wake up and face reality-only when the streets are made of gold will hate/prejudice/racism be eradicated.Fred Douglas said, "right,is of no sex,truth is of no color,God is the Father of us all and all we are brethren." so it's not really a SKIN problem but a SIN problem!! The heart of the problem is the problem of the heart! Spugeon said, "Beware of no man more than yourself,we carry our worst enemies within us." Even people imprisoned in hell have no doors or bolts on their cells.(I,we,humans) are the problem and the only absolute solution is JESUS!--customer 1 and 3 pause to munch deep into their spicy lunchtime meal gulping as quickly as possible to get the first word back in! Customer 3 is victorious and continues; "you have to admit, the media and goo-goo Hollywood protect, conceal,ignore and concoct all lies and deceit on the cash funded pedestal that they put Obama on. A pedestal where Marx snickers proudly at the progressive propaganda of 'change'! how insane!! They must all be patients in nurse Ratched's ward! He's the first dark shade of melanin president in America's history! Since America is a Democratic Republic it was our genius Founding Fathers who were able to install checks & balances that eventually dissolved the chains and injustices. We are all now free-all people! Hallelujah!" Customer1 nods in agreement adding;" yeah,you know they blame America and call it a racist country. Well the proof is that America is not racist BUT that there are RACIST in America and also all around the globe.This is the theme of our main man Mr. Douglas. He did say after his reappraisal of America";

ITALY-15

'my rethinking of radical change in my opinion of America.. The signers of the Declaration of Independence were brave great men. Statesman,patriots,heroes. The Constitution interpreted as it ought to be interpreted as a glorious liberty document and I defy the presentation of a single pro-slavery clause in it. On the other hand it will be found to contain principles and purposes entirley hostile to the existence of slavery. I know of no soil better adapted to the growth of reform than American soil. I know no country where the conditions for affecting great changes in the settled order of things for the development of right ideas of liberty and humanity are more favorably than here in these United States. The Constitution,Declaration of Independence, and sentiments of the founders of the Republic give us a platform broad enough and strong enough to support the most comprehensive plans for the freedom and elevation of all people of this country without regard to COLOR, CLASS,CLIMATE.I love the pure peaceable and impartial Christianity of Christ (of this land).I therefore hate the corrupt slaveholding women-whipping cradle plundering partial and hypocritical Christianity of this land'

Customer 1 proudly exudes factual facts from his history major memory,

"Let's remember the first Republican president, Abraham Lincoln, who Frederick Douglas was quoted as saying, 'Abe Lincoln is the one man… to whom we are more indebted for a united nation and for American liberty than to any other…he's the greatest statesman that ever presided over the destinies of this Republic.' So, it was Lincoln and the abolitionists who were a high percentage of whites that represent symbolically in Frederick Douglas's statement as the impartial pure peaceable America.This was the America that Douglas defended, identified with and loved. And throughout the true balance of history(delete all revisionist narratives) -most of the Democrat party represent Frederick Douglas slaveholding-Jim Crow-Segregationist-women whipping- cradle plundering partial hypocritical America. This America-he abhorred and despised because the Democrats' policies consistently reflected this ideology and was in opposition and conflict to what Douglas believed, wrote and preached."

Customer 3 interrupts respectfully, "hey, let's get back to Obama. Come on, cut me some slack, he scolded CEOs and their jet motives and then with elitist gall jets in a chef 860 miles from St. Louis to make specially designed pizza. I wonder what was the size of that carbon footprint from those pies and somewhere somehow US taxpayers pockets were picked.Iknow,i know what some people say, 'oh,he's soooo elegant with his speech.But little do they realize that he's a teleprompter addict who wears non-transparent suits with missing American flag pins covered over by a trench coat of only donkey color.His grey shirts and czars muscle an agenda flexing into our bedrooms, kitchens,garage,attics, crawl space and bathrooms with Orwellian hammer and sickle eyes. Under his watch the policy was issued to silence and regulate radio speech and also to document and to flag opposing email views. We have to be moral when it comes to health care and then quotes principles from the Bible. But this,from the guy who covered and ashamedly hid the cross of Jesus and refused the national day of prayer that was to be held at the White House. He fights to allow the murder of infants for any reason, at any time(right up to the 9th month) even if they're born alive from a botched abortion-

'Doctors,nurses don't touch those blobs of fetal choice, I want it lawful not to care for them but let them die! That's right, leave the room and ignore that innocent human and his/her heartbeat'-

and on top of that he wants to force taxpayers to pay for the murders even if your pro-life.

ITALY- 16

In the meantime, his lobbyist are not only getting fatter but their pockets definitely have obese love handles.

                    Please!

        Power!   And!   Agenda!

Duh!

Could that be his only motive??

Do you actually think he's gonna allow his daughters to experience what he and his cabinet and his party push for behind their closed doors to force on the public??

Wait,a sec customer 1,I'm almost done." customer 3 proudly demanded and politely SHHH'D, as customer 1 tried to vocalize some more pertinent facts.

"OH, and how dare the average American go to a constitutional town hall meeting to plead their constitutional right to constitutionally oppose his policies. If they do then his media mongrels and party people will call them anti-american and label them Nazis. You do know that his policies and party support vehemently crave more government promising that this is the better way,only way- bow tie anointed bureaucratic controllers. Of course they forget what happens in history as history repeats and reveals--- that more government eventually produces the clash of classes recycling tyrants or in this case a soft tyrant who was born in Honolulu. I still sweat to make ends meet!! (on a positive note,[C major],in life don't sweat the petty things but be careful not to pet the sweaty things).ok, now where was I before i rudely interrupted myself-- oh yeah, and now for my sarcasm- he's such a great Commander in Chief, i never saw limpness have you when

Kim Jong il said to Barak,
> "You whistle- I missile!"

He bows to sheiks yet snubs up his nose against Israel. He goes on apology tours erasing the terminology 'war on terror' to PC Muslim appeasement heights. Terrorists are gaining more legal protection as he strips America of our shields. Under his scepter reign

Insane ideologies
Pause
Putrid

Headshakes;Hollow cowards use red herring to attack CIA tactics which everyone was in on which protected USA and saved untold lives-

Government 'can't' force a woman to give birth to a child!!

So ABORT/MURDER at free will and as often

BUT not too far in the future, the Government 'can' force a woman NOT to give birth to a child!! Hey, why not imitate the Chinese 2 limit rule --that sounds cool.

A few more things before i'm distracted by nature

1. The president and his family goes on vacation during an intense period of crisis and war and the worm media says basically - relax and enjoy the vacation Obama's but when president Bush and his family went on vacation during what the puss media interpreted as crisis and war-- the outcry was basically-- how dare he- how irresponsible, how inconsiderate- how shameful!!

2. A poster of Barry with the face of the 'Joker' painted on his face is circulated and the outcries were rampant of racism,that it's mean,deplorable! But the almost exact same poster and 'Joker' face was painted on the face of Bush and its whispered political satire and poetic license."

3. President Bush falls over what would normally be a human tongue stutter but he's attacked as 'stupid' a dunce but President Obama spurts out that, "the 57 states-blah blah blah" and this same media is suddenly mute.

ITALY-17

4. The media blames Bush for nature's flood but this same media AGAIN is willfully mute-no comment- we consciously suppress- Solyndra(GREEN) Gate-Holder's 'Fast&Furious'plot- stimulus taxes('cause they're the 'Taxman, yeeaahh,they're the Taxman)-stimulus class warfare-Occupy Wall street protest(get over it- we agree, there's corruption everywhere/since all time- stop the millionaire bashing(how come you don't mention that they are 1% of the population BUT pay 50% of our TAXES!).

5. This same media who all of a sudden left their tongues inside their bowels when Bush and Gulliani were compared to Hitler YET this same media,journalist and celebrities all joined together for a unified agonizing cry of triumph over Hank Jr's termination from MNF because he compared Hitler to Obama even though Hank used OBVIOUS symbolic literary language which by the way is also based on his (and the Constitution's) free speech rights."

Finally customer 1 and 3 sauntered closer to one of the park's benches away from the lure of another pound of cholesterol joy but not before they announced angrily to the world almost closer than the knit duo harmonies of the Everly Brothers;

"HEY, U'Z - cubed squash minds of goo-foolish dolt brainwashed slanted yoyoZ- just be fair-just be honest-!! NO slant-NO dilute- NO bias-!! Just report both parties or any party-EQUALLY-EVENALLY! Heed Lennon's voice--'Just gimme some truth-all I want is the truth-I'm sick and tired of hearing things from uptight short sided narrow minded hypocrites-I've had enough of reading things by neurotic, psychotic, pigheaded POLITICIANS"-and we'll insert here additional lyrics as if Paul was helping John-' journalist media molls twitching in their sleep-drooling on their gonzo/tabloid pillows with the incantation-'Don't let the facts get in the way of a good story[translated-'false narrative}'

-----------if only that fly on the White House wall could raise its tinie tiny halteres gyrating to testify that the

deepstateshadowgovernmentalongwiththeirhookermedia

actively participated/initiated/ignored

-The attempted silent Coup of #45 under #44 as he(44) and his sly specks conspired to entangle #45 sowing seeds and roots of lies/ manipulation as factually exposed under Spygate - no justice as Hillary deletes over 30,000 emails &/ bleach performance

(failed)impeachment based on partisan hate
-even smear tactics on even #45 supporters like Kanye-Ye-
Yet again the mute button has been pushed as

NOcollusionNOobstructionNOukraineNOquidproquo became a reality.Trump won/wins and also he's draining the swamp and dosen't cower to the PC police and DNC media.

Hitler said,"if you tell a big lie and tell it frequently,it will be believed... and through clever and constant application of propaganda-people can be made to see paradise as hell and consider the most wretched sort of life as paradise." yet most of the DemocRATS-the left- the mainstream 'fake'media-most of hollywood continue to frequently constantly apply the lie that there WAS-collusion-obstruction-ukraine-quid pro quo!!

Hitler would be like a proud dad watching his children mature into their narrated paradise.

Hey Who was that future time travelerInterlude warning?? (da Vinci wrote that the water you touch in a river is the last of what has passed and the first of that which comes, so it is with present time) So back to the present Italy's gonna Right about now gonna change this subject go-oooooo ahhhh

ITALY-18

The- oo00's & aaHH's
Are like the intensity of extreme sports because if you could
Check
This out, literally
Check
Like a
Check
Mark formation, from Italy's viewpoint-then--------Adulation
Glides blue sky perfect Strides true high Geese
    Like chocolate sprinkles on maple L'unifolie creme glacee
Intelligent design Definite Check Mark Check
It out- "oooo!!" "ahhhh!!"-----like a silent nishiki kamuro display--
a dense elegant Baroque of the Four Seasons, Toccata and Fugue
BURSTING
Gracefully into a classical glittering tail of

                    Eine Kleine Nachtmusik
                    Rondo Alla Tunca
                    Jupiter
                    Into into wait wait aspettare
                    Into what looks like

Yes
Its forming into, yes, yes, could it be
WOW, Stradivari's vintage instrument

Flying with flapping active feathers

Amazing massage

Then shift

Arrowhead

Drift

Poetry

Flight Competitors-- worthy of the whirling twist turn

Instant troop murmuration

of all individual Starlings' swarm decisions.

Oh no,man,onion sauce has officially consummated the main forest of Italy's tan leg.

Question: does Ireland boast

Of loving, living, obeying

CHRIST,

Of being born from above of repenting of his spotted crimson soul to be cleansed into pure wool only by the pierced side of the Nazarene-of being saved & written in the Lamb's book of life justified only by the Son of David from His victory over the grave????????????

well, does he???????????????????????????????-Proverb 20:9(NIV) who can say, "I have kept my heart pure;I am clean and without sin."Jeremiah 13:23(ESV), can the Ethiopian change his skin or the leopard his spots? Philippians 3:9 Is he or any of us found in Christ Righteousness and not our own(NKJV)- BECAUSE Isaiah 64:6 says- we are all as an unclean thing and all our righteousness are as filthy rags(NKJV)…! SO-Galatian 2:21 says; do not frustrate/set aside the grace of God, for if righteousness could be gained through the law/deeds/works then Christ died for nothing.(NKJV&AMP)

IRELAND-7

However,verily,moreover, i have not read Italy's last episode in its entirety

But

There's -"booze in the blender and soon it will render me concocted into Buffettville"-and the second i spake thus with poetical prattle on paper

with Poe's quill pen

   mind you,Woolf and Plath were in his chambers-all fondled intellectually by Woody Allen

"Hope is the thing with feathers? Nephew from Zurich? Hope keeps me alive. Such tyranny is time, a prime, a John Prine forsooth.

   I miss my daughter. Her 1st words at 10 months old were,"ha-da"! Well, hello baby, daddys here! I'm crying. Do not tempt the Lord, for His sword strikes with mercy, love, and force…

   coerce the verse when i lack the Passion, i am behooved to smooth another's pain again, always, always, in whatever fashion. I must end this episode, leaving Italy to a brusque rebuttal, and therefore, appendix and he's giving me agita around my appendix! As I penned in previous writings, circa

1996

"If the morrow I wake, looking stone cold in retrospect, all the excuses fail to excuse, for all my words have been written."

now,2009 or 2019 or ????, and much traumatic stress later, if the Lord that Italy speaks of desires me in His chessboard fiat to forever burn and suffer, then as is such.However, I have repented my sins invariable to the omnipotent/omniscient One. They must be repented- since- the white collar 'father' told me that they were when he slid the tiny window closed, told me to exit the confessional and recite/pray 2 'Our Fathers',

3 'Hail Marys or was it 3 'Our Fathers' and 9 'Hail Marys'? I have lived 32 years procuring to live up to my name and I need not a mere mortal to inform, let alone, put in print that a hell is imminent. The sins committed against me, well, Confucian reciprocity is what you will get from the get,

scars.

Turning the other cheek, Jesus may well have done, while in pure dictatorial knowledge, understanding that His Immortal Pappy will place/toss/indulge Himself, made in own image with Choice/Beelzebub as constant scapegoat, in that cute hell-fire;which is as much a contradiction and noxious ignorance as calling me a friend and proverbial pig in the same sentence.You,Italy,with your kindness to me and a shy pretence of respect have hurt me deeply and I was already irrevocably deterred from being a simple and happy individual. I am as loyal as you may ask and pray for in this valley so misguided by an irascible and sexually explicit Holy Book of rules and vices. Hitler proved that if you could burn a book, then you could burn a human. Judge not lest ye be judged. You have hurt me, mate, I walk alone, in all company, with the Lord.

Pater noster, qui es, in caelis, sanctificetur, nomen tuum. Adveniat regnum tuum. Fiat voluntas tua, sicut in caelo, et in terra. Panem nostrum quoticanum da nobis hodie. Et dimitte nobis debita nosta, sicut et nos dimmittimus debitoribus nostris. Et ne nos inducas in Tentationem: Sed Libero Nos a Malo. Amen.

"Alas, two souls dwell in my breast"- Goethe

ITALY-19

Just because my ears are shaped like potato chips doesn't make me wise.Any saltiness from me is from the sprinkling spice of God Himself off of me onto those fields the Lord will hopefully harvest into His barn. Italy will not regress-rehash-reiterate-recount-revoke-retrieve, prior evidence of Ireland's spiritual state. Ireland's bark speaks for the bite that shreds open the eyes to the truth. I'm not spewing Dogberry's BLATHERSKITE but only slicing with Paraclete's perspicacious Sword. Hey, it's obvious- if someone picks from a tree and thorns fill the basket then that was OBVIOUSLY not a Spirit sealed peach tree!! Remember!! Ireland could not answer the kindergarten basics of how--why--where--of salvation based solely in Scripture,based solely from Jesus' lips and the apostles doctrine. So when he quotes, recites scriptures as only a recitation,then he's not wheat in God's barn!!

Some might say/or think---further/farther--And yet one letter difference--So don't be so picky perfect about Ireland's testimony(verbal&action)!! Some say/think it's a conundrum --further/farther---notoriously confused some say/think---- But the

English language(analogy-Bible) rules objectively and dictates each and every single meaning as to the context of who would be possessing the true professing of further/farther!!

However with the Bible it's not a profession BUT a possessing of faith! Ireland- 'knows of' the Creator(remember his 'Thread'p8-9) but the Bible guidance map commands all to 'know' Him and make Him 'known'- NOT 'know of' but only to 'know' is the true relationship that Jesus the Shepherd desires for His sheep. Sure-Italy cut deep into Ireland's heart. It's not me. I blame the Bible!! A blame Italy would die for. The Bible; that double edge sword confronts-demolishes- Human,conceit,pride,worldviews-

    Slices
dices

Spiritual impotence, false beliefs, doctrinal deceptions, cultic persuasion, ALL- exactly at the same moment during that sword slice- is a crystal clear mirror reflecting- condemning- revealing- Our lost dead sin stained souls-- convicting us to look at ourselves as it demands(and we don't like to be demanded upon) our allegiance And

If we don't commit, then there's no second chance. UM (and i am not chanting OM), so it's really God and His Word that agitates/ aggravates/cuts you-that's the issue.But for now, we'll

go with the 'me' issue. In a way, it is-me-in a sense-because it is God using-me-! I'm His shofar as His Breath flows through-me-! Hopefully- i reach out with open arms and it's with the Carpenter's embrace. The hurt you say i hurt you is in reality the salve that's kind and loving. Salt preserves and heals yet applied to the wounded(like a wounded soul)

it STINGS.STINGS for the good. Open rebuke is better than love concealed.

QUESTION??Would I give you 62 trick birthday candles to blow out if you were consumed by drowning last stage vile curdling emphysema??

Would I take you up to the edge of the exosphere for an amateur airplane jump and give you a parachute filled with six dozen X-Box 360 Kinect sensors?? Would I, knowing that you and your daughter were cocooned in rem stage on the second floor as an insane fire engulfs the first floor, continue on my cell focused on the daily lottery shrugging my shoulders at your fatal fate??Jude 1:23 commands me to save others snatching those out of the fire-(NASB) as if they were dangling over the eternal lake of torment!! So- I obey! Now for the 'judge not lest you be judged' comment- why do unbelievers or the biblical illiterate proudly puff out this verse as if they're winning in debate forum when in actuality they're falling off a tricycle onto shards of fallacy glass. CONTEXT- CONTEXT-CONTEXT!! 'They' forget or don't 'know' Jesus' command for His soldiers to 'judge righteously'!

ITALY-20

Test! Prove! Examine! EVERY--thing! EVERY--one!

Would a kirpan under Italy's AO-DAI remain silent as the Pol Pot regime rapes his daughters??

Or could it be unbeknownst to Ireland,that the 'T' word is intimidating his temperature,to whatever degree-partial or extreme!

T

O

L

E

R

A

N

C

E

!!!

Word! T! T-word! Buzzword in contemporary newscast, entertainment, radio, media galaxy, popular discourse! TOLERANCE! Pressure of postmodernism has squeezed 'T' into another definition. A smokescreen propaganda to formally and fully affirm practically every alternative lifestyle,worldview, and religion. Instead of 'T' of which the true virtue of showing patience, kindness, longsuffering, and forbearance, toward people we disagree with and not deleting absolute truth from the equation. 'T',today, twist our arms behind our backs to hold any opinion or belief that you like and at the same time you must refrain from criticizing others their ideas and you are forbidden to publicly disapprove of anyone's behavior or value system, especially on moral or biblical grounds.'T', now,says, never suggest that one belief system or standard of righteousness is universally true and binding on everyone. If the truth is the truth but doesn't itch the ears then its considered offensive-you are then labeled,

I

N

T

O

L

E

R

A

N

T

!!!

Tolerance- now a familiar rhyme;

Every voice

   Every opinion

      It's no choice

         Demand dominion

Equal treatment.

Every aberration expects to be formally validated. Every form of behavior or misbehavior is supposed to be accepted as normal. No matter how divergent or discordant two or more opinions,ides, beliefs,religions might be, no matter how bizarre or irrational their worldviews are, we, definitely, are supposed to embrace and treat them ALL with equal respect, credibility, value, and deemed as its own truth, therefore-- true!!??

ITALY-21

Ahhhhh-

  but let's just see how

T

O

L

E

R

A

N

T   these new 'tolerant' Webster REdefining REvisionists really are?? If I stood up in a public forum or even fiveum which was covered by MSNBC-CNN-the NY Times and the rest of the slant media and Hollywood, etc, et hoc genus omne, and declared out loud that Jesus and ONLY Jesus is the only ONE true Messiah- God-Creator-Savior- the ONLY way- only TRUTH- only life and quoted His teachings that verified what i just preached and continue with His commands like; "whosoever, does not believe, obey, and follow Me and does not repent is condemned into an eternal lake of fire of mental and physical torment and all other religions are false! (Mark 16:16/John 3:15-16,36 & 14:6)

You know exactly what would instantly happen--

> They would spew their dogmatically 'INTOLERANT' vomit
> to try and suffocate me and then stomp the living absolutes
> out of me!! to achieve their new standard of TOLERANT.

Every distinction between truth and error must be erased!
Relativism now lives.

Absolutes now dead.

Anything can claim truth as long as it is not exclusive, universal absolute truth. They say there are no absolutes!! WOW- they seem so sure and absolute!

I wonder? Would they crucify Love Incarnate with His response to this 'T' trend?

Examine Christ pattern as He relates to truth and you judge righteously!!

Jesus did not engage in endless conversations about subjective interpretation of scripture

Or

Agree to disagree

on foundational doctrines. Jesus

did not give equal time to spurious teachers or try to find common ground with theological opponents. Jesus

Voice was peace if possible truth at all cost. Jesus

confronted and blatantly exposed and rebuked error-lies-hypocrisy!! Jesus

pointedly refused to contribute to any sense of religious ecumenical unity. Jesus

Was

Is

Uncompromising, unyielding, and

I
N
T
O
L
E
R
A
N
T with false,deceptive, doctrine-actually anything false!!

ITALY-22

Jesus

Was

Is

firm and relentless for the truth NEVER lenient towards wrong, erroneous beliefs.

Jesus

T

O

L

E

R

A

N

C

E

Was

Is

Exemplified in His patience,compassion,love,and service to all kinds of people with no regard to social standing(or sitting). Jesus Correcting,exposing,confronting,challenging error

Was

Is

One of the most loving acts that anyone can project.(yo,grazie John MacArthur Jr. for the above inspiration)

Italy detaches himself momentarily from his endeavor to press lips to his beloved because I am my beloved and my beloved is mine, that is his-his own personal shulamite queen-Milca/Mira.

There   i'm back

Now for the good news.just as simple and quick as me saying-"gospel"- at Veterans Park

fellowship feast of the gathering of the saints from Emmanuel Community Church, through the escape of cow soul from the active propane grill,through the exclusive smoke where various aerial bugs do the jitterbug, through the festive flavored air of fennel seed sausage clinging to #30 applied lotion and the clink of Italy and Ireland's aluminum encased carbonated beverages,through resonating exploiting ears--oh,yeah,the good news, angels shared pieces of manna birth cake-, because an adopted infant was spanked awake by the quickening of the Comforter. YES-that's right-you heard(actually read) what I said(typed)------Ireland--- received the LORD Jesus and Him crucified/resurrected/returning and also confessed his sin stained soul as needing to be cleansed and made righteous forever only by Jeus and His victorious propitiatory sacrifice on Calvary. He will now miss the 'second death' and receive some hidden manna and a new name written on his own white stone.

Welcome brother(cuz/bro/bro/cuz) into the kingdom-from the guttermost to the uttermost.Soon we'll be clinking glasses to

drink of the juice of the vine at the marriage supper of the Lamb. So to all,heed- an ephemeral eternity that will begin quicker than it takes that- light train-to travel across a single nucleon-
ALL ABOARD!!

So be found in His righteousness and let our hope be built on nothing less than Jesus blood and righteousness. Since Yeshua carried His sheep on eagles wings and brought us to Himself it's NOW time for a little

R&R(Risen&Returning)!

IRELAND-8

Well God works miracles-well,let me rephrase-

He rescued me from the wrath to come,now, that's the miracle and

So i must recant -Ireland 4-(yeah,just review it- you'll realize why i recant)

How ridiculous, now that I've been enlightened by the Spirit, of what i was thinking in my episode back then but a dead man can't breathe on his own. I'm eternally grateful that the 'Hound of Heaven' pursued me, rescued me, sacrificed for me- HALLELUJAH!!

Ora capisco

When Italy was saying

Capisci

To the only Way for salvation!! Now i'll enjoy

Paul's dilemma-

      Ecstatic polyphonic

Oh

What a wake up remedy

Oh

What stinging adrenaline

Pump up

To   remain?

To   depart?

                    Equal crave to expand the body to hug the Head>

Hey

For now

bisect my choice, and swoon me into the voracious juice of both!

I pray your decision will be equally difficult!! Oh,

What swwwwwweeeeet difficulty!

I have an urge to quote-who i've come to study and enjoy, TA-DA, the

'Prince of Preachers'; "I believe that every particle of dust that dances in

the sunbeam does not move an atom more or less than God wishes…"

So until we meet in the clouds

I-me-we-you-he-she-they-us(and the rest of pronoun euphoria)

need to imitate the following combo/be a,

   ballistic

   e

   r   p

   Edelweiss

   a   r

   n   a

   t

   e

      ---ding-ding--now serving--- haiku sandwich

                    to every purpose

                    there is a season and dust

                    and beams are reason.

                    nonpareil sweets

                    unparalleled chocolate treats

                    sprinkled coins,indulge.

                    life is a hyphen

                    lyric impressionism

                    Live-googoo,volta.

NARRATOR DUE

We hope you have enjoyed the show

We're sorry but it's time to go

We'd like to thank you once again

It's getting very near the end

Soooooooooooooooooooooooo

               We who are alive

say

to all students of every language using your retina from cornea

foveal/peripheral vision scanning these pages

then sending our souls

A Thousand Years Hence

5 words (maybe 17-ish)

as a message that we shall not pass along-we/us&you in----

SYZYGY, yes

SYZYGY -

        what

        U think we're gonna end

        With a period

and in the end

the love you take

is equal to

the love you make

Printed in the United States
by Baker & Taylor Publisher Services